Ten Tips to Stand Out In a Crowded Market

Put Your Resume to Work

Kristin Starzyk

ISBN-13: 978-1516979370
ISBN-10: 1516979370

Table of Contents

Introduction

Getting ready to make the jump into your first career out of school? Planning on moving out of state? Making a career change? There are lots of items to keep in mind for your resume depending on your situation. For each of the situations listed above, there are different areas on your resume that should stand out to show that you are the ideal candidate for the position. This book will help get your resume into the condition that it should be in to not only meet the standards of the interviewers, but to surpass their expectations.

Before we jump into the real nitty-gritty of how to best present your resume, there are a couple items that I would like to emphasize, and will continue to emphasize throughout. Spell check and proofreading are key! Yes, I know that all word processing software (i.e. Microsoft Word) has a spell check and picks up on a lot of grammatical errors; however, a "manger" and a "manager" don't mean quite the same thing. While a manger will be a good place to stay dry, including this as a key word on your resume for a manager position will not show that you are detail oriented. This is just one example of why you need to proofread, as spell check won't always pick this up.

It's also very important to stay true to who you are and your skills while writing your resume. If you are applying to a position and have the leadership skills or education required to fill a position, but are missing say, for example, the experience sought for certain software, don't state you have knowledge of this software just to try to make yourself seem more qualified. It will come out at some point that you do not possess this knowledge, and this will not look good on your part. Instead, you should just build your character up and present yourself in a way that the company will want to hire you anyways.

Now, let's jump into some of the basics and get you on your way to making your ideal resume and jumpstarting that career!

Tip #1 – Come up with a Rough Outline for Your Resume

Updating your resume, let alone beginning a resume from scratch, is never a fun or easy thing to do. The process can be very time consuming and tedious, particularly for those who hate talking about themselves. Don't get frustrated! This process does not, and for that matter *should not*, be completed in one day.

The best starting place, no matter where your resume currently stands, is to come up with an outline of yourself.

The first thing you will want to complete is a list of any jobs / work experience that you have had in the past. For this step, you will just want to note the name of the place, the position you held, and the dates you worked there. Leave some space next to or below each of these positions. You don't need to use an exact date (i.e. March 6, 20X5), you can just list the dates by the month and year (i.e. March 20X5). Whether you have worked at a Fortune 500 company, a fast food joint, or a simple volunteer job, all of these positions are important and should be included during this step. They will all show that you have had to maintain a work schedule, work with clients and co-workers, etc. I will get into this in a little more detail later on. If you have not had an "official position," don't rule out things you might have done in your free time. Babysitting, helping out at the school store, or being involved in certain organizations can also help to show the same type of characteristics as an "official position" would, so don't leave these out when you are jotting down your list.

The second thing that you will want to do is jot down some of the key responsibilities you had while holding this position. At this point in time, don't worry about sentences or grammar or anything more than the tasks you completed. Some examples of what to jot down are as follows:

- Worked register
- Customer service
- Scheduling
- Prepared financial statements
- Kept children calm

We will get into the best manner of describing these items later on. Now it is just important to think about the things you did while holding each of these positions. Don't worry about whether you think the items were super important or not; the best thing is to write down whatever comes to mind first. It can always be modified or removed later on.

Now that you have listed out any positions you have held for jobs and their specific tasks, you will want to do the same for any volunteer organizations that you have been in. You should list the same items as you did above for these positions – name of the organization, titles held (if any), dates you were involved, and any tasks you had for this position(s). If you only attended one meeting or volunteered for the organization once, I may put an asterisk (*) next to it just as a reminder for when you are reviewing which items to include on your resume.

The next thing that you will want to do when coming up with your outline is to come up with a list of any skills you may have gained from any of the positions or volunteer organizations you were in. These skills can be a wide range of items and can include technical (i.e. computer software) or behavioral skills (i.e. managerial or leadership). Some examples of possible skills are as follows:

- If you were a manager, you may have had to attend various leadership seminars or conferences. This could be included as a leadership skill.
- If you had to work every day using a certain software (i.e. Microsoft Word or Excel), you could include this as a technical skill.

- If you were a babysitter / nanny and required certain certifications (i.e. CPR), this would be something to include here.
- If you speak more than one language, this can also be something you can list out here.

For each of the skills that you have listed, you will then want to review them to determine if it would be appropriate to give a level to the skill. This will let your potential employer or interviewer gain a better understanding as to where your knowledge or expertise falls for these items. Keep in mind that not everything listed needs to have a level of expertise. A level of expertise – i.e. basic, intermediate, advanced, expert – is more important when it comes to technical skills than it would be for behavioral skills. For example, if you list that you have leadership skills, you don't necessarily need to list a level, just that you have attended leadership training.

For further reference or guide as to examples of how to list out your jobs and the respective responsibilities you had, see Appendix A. For further reference or guide as to examples of skills, see Appendix B.

Tip #2 – Know Your Audience

Before any new board game or television show comes out, the producers have done intense research and market studies to determine who the target audience or users of their product are going to be. They want to make sure that they have not only identified them, but have brainstormed some ideas of ways to stand out and be a must buy product or must watch show. Without making the efforts to advertise their product in such a way to intrigue their audience and demonstrate some sort of value, it can be very hard to sell their product. Just think about how many board games and TV shows are currently out their waiting to be bought or watched.

This same concept goes for you when you are beginning with your job search. While it may seem like an odd notion, you are the product and the potential company you are applying to is your audience. Just like the producers of the game or show, you must show your future employer what makes you stand out and why they should "buy," or hire you, instead of the many other options out there.

While it is possible to just walk-in off the street and apply to a company, it is always good to do some background research on the place of business. Not only will it give you an overall feel for the company and whether you may like it or not, but it will also demonstrate to the company that you have a higher level of interest in the company. There are many different ways that you can go about learning about a company; the easiest and best starting point would be the internet.

Everything can be found on the internet these days and the best starting place to begin your background research is typically the main company website. See below for the main items that you will want to familiarize yourself with and the reason why this may be beneficial:

Company History / Mission: Sometimes these two sections are combined onto one page, other times they will be found on separate pages. These sections will be the best spot to go to gain an understanding about the culture of the company and why you might want to work here. The person in charge of the website will have chosen the important facts to include in the company history that led to the company being founded and the building blocks that have kept them in business. This will give you an idea of the key players in management that may interview you. Going along with this, the company mission will give you a look into the key values of the company. This is typically a one sentence statement that describes the main goal that the founders of the company had in mind as to why the company exists and the overall manner in which they want to keep the company operating. Below are some examples of mission statements for some well-known companies to give you an idea of the type of statements:

- McDonald's brand mission is to be our customers' favorite place and way to eat and drink.[1]
- Amazon's mission is to be Earth's most customer-centric company, where customers can find and discover anything they might want to buy online, and endeavors to offer its customers the lowest possible prices.[2]
- State Farm's mission is to help people manage the risks of everyday life, recover from the unexpected, and realize their dreams.[3]

Services: Always take some time to review the services that the company has listed on their website. Just because a company is in the industry or field that you want to focus on, doesn't mean that they will provide the services to clients that are typical of other companies in that industry.

---

[1] http://www.aboutmcdonalds.com/mcd/our_company/mission_and_values.html
[2] http://www.amazon.jobs/working/working-amazon
[3] https://www.statefarm.com/about-us/company-overview/company-profile/mission

What do I mean by this? Take an insurance company for example, you could be coming from Company A and looking at Company B. Company A may have provided services for home, auto, insurance, and boats, allowing you for multiple areas to focus on; however, Company B could just specialize in home insurance. This will help provide you with the knowledge that when you are describing tasks completed at Company A, you may want to place more emphasis on what you did in this one industry (home insurance) as this will be the main focus for Company B.

If you would prefer having a variety of areas to work in, it's important to know that Company B doesn't provide this option. You don't want to spend the time tailoring your resume for a company that isn't aligned with what you want. And worse off, you don't want to go into an interview without this vital background knowledge and find out that you wasted both your and the company's time.

Career Page: While the information on this page varies depending on the company, this page is important as it is setup to give potential candidates an outside view of what a typical day in the life of an employee will be. On here you can usually find job descriptions of what to expect as an intern, full-time staff or part-time staff. This will also show any community organizations that the company, or individuals within the company, is involved with. Another typical item that you will be able to find here are pictures from previous events that the company has hosted for their employees. These will help give you an idea of whether or not there is a focus on life outside of work. You will also be able to see if the Company is involved in any of the same Organizations that you may be in.

Job Postings: Take the time to look over the job postings, if any, listed on the company website. You will want to focus on the wording and key terms that are used by the company throughout the posting. These key terms are something that you will want to make a note of, particularly those terms used when the company is describing the characteristics they are looking for in their ideal candidate. You will want to use as many of these key terms that apply to you as possible. By doing so, you will help align yourself with exactly what the company is looking for; just be sure that you are appropriately characterizing yourself. We'll get into this in a little more detail in Tip #8 – Impressing v. Exaggerating.

Something to keep in mind is that you don't want to just focus on the main company website. While this will definitely help you gain a very good overview, this will only provide you with a limited viewpoint of the company. Since it is created and maintained by the company, only the better parts of company and its services will be listed. You will also want to do a general internet search. You don't need to read every article, but at least glance at the headlines. This will help to determine if the company is associated with good press or bad press, and help you determine the type of company / reputation you may be getting yourself into. Social media, while not your typical news headline, is also a good place to look at to gain an inside look at the employees, culture of the firm and possible events the company puts on.

Just remember to jot down key points as you are going through and reading each of these areas. These key points will be the guide to help you tailor your resume towards the company, not just when commenting regarding your previous experience, but in your skills and any volunteer experiences as well.

Tip #3 – Know and Understand the Position

Before you begin to update your resume, it is vital that you not only know the job description that you are applying to, but that you also understand the position. Why is this step so important? You don't want to waste time preparing a resume and getting ready for an interview for a job that you are going to hate from day one. You also don't want to waste the time of the company who could have interviewed a candidate that was more excited for the position. More importantly, you don't want to have your resume geared towards, for example, a supervisory position when the company is looking for more of a team focus. While you may be fine with a position in either role, the company may not be able to tell this from your resume. As a result, this could rule you out of the running for the position before you even had a chance to talk with the company.

How do you go about learning more regarding a position? There are several manners in which this can be completed depending on how you are applying for a position:

Through the Website: The easiest place to go for information on a position is by looking at the Company website. Most places have a spot on their website specifically related to a career with them. This may be in the "About Us" section, "Contact Us" section or in its own separate "Career" section. Typically, this will have a detailed listing of all job postings that the Company currently has to offer. This should include a description of the general responsibilities and qualifications for each opening.

Check to see if the position focuses on any particular service or industry. Use this information to explore and read about that section on the website – typically under a "Services" section. This may help to give you a better idea as to how much might be involved with regards to certain responsibilities, or whether you think you will have the appropriate qualifications to be successful with the position. See Appendix C for some examples of specific items that you might want to keep in mind while reviewing the website.

Through the Company: Yes, it may sound like a crazy concept, but if you still feel like you don't fully understand the responsibilities and requirements of the job position, there is always one place you can go that definitely knows the job. You are always welcome to contact the company directly.

- Send the Company an email via its website - there is typically a contact us section. You can click on this and send a quick message to ask for a representative of the Company to contact you. When you do this, be sure to include the full title of the position that you are applying for and a quick summary of what you are looking for from them – i.e. an overview of the position, expectations, general responsibilities, etc.
- Call the Company's main number and ask to speak to the human resources or recruiting department. Again, you want to make sure you fully explain why you are calling, and include the title of the position, your name, and the best call back number.

While this is probably the best manner to get specific questions answered regarding the position, keep in mind that this phone call or email is a representation of you. Don't just send a quick email without re-reading or editing it. If there are several misspellings or grammatical errors, this could cause the Company to think you are not detailed oriented even though you may be. Also, you want to be sure that you have some specific questions set aside to ask the company representative. See Appendix C for some examples of specific questions that you could ask to get the conversation started or help you to continue it if you find you're not sure what else to ask.

Through a Recruiter: If you are able to find the position through a recruiter, they are always a good resource to bounce questions off of relating to the job and Company. They will be in direct contact with key personnel at the Company. It is also likely that they will have had previous experiences dealing with the Company, so they may be able to answer questions relating to specific qualifications expected. You can also review Appendix C for some examples of specific questions that you could ask to get the conversation started or help you to continue it if you find you're not sure what else to ask.

Now that you have read the position and have obtained an understanding of what is expected of you, you should determine whether your thoughts and hopes of what you expect from the position are in alignment with everything you learned. If it seems like the position is something that you will enjoy doing and are willing to take the time to learn any new skills, then you should continue with the process of updating your resume and applying to the position. Jot down any key words or qualifications you noted while going through the website or having your phone calls to use in your resume and help make it stand out.

If you are still unsure about the position, you may be better off giving it a day or two to think about the position some more. If needed, you could always contact the Company again to see if you could speak to an employee in a similar position to gain a better understanding of a typical day.

Tip #4 – Use an Appropriate Writing Style

While the content of your resume is important, how you write it is vital as well. Even if your past experiences are perfect compared to what your potential employer is seeking, you could be turned down for a position based on the writing style chosen for your resume. One of the biggest problem areas surrounding writing style relates to the tense of writing. The other big problem area is the formality in which a resume has been written. We will go into more detail about these below. Other areas that we will touch upon relate to: grammar and being aware of the industry in which you are seeking a position.

Tense Usage: Your choice of tense – past, present, future – is important when describing your jobs and the tasks that you had while in each position. Why, you might ask? This will provide the employer with a rough idea as to how recently you were using certain skills or completing certain tasks. In addition, the employer will be able to gauge how your responsibility levels and role at your company have increased. For example, if your resume for a retail position includes "maintained a clean and organized clothing display" as well as "supervise that all tasks are being completed, including an organized display," then a reader of your resume will be able to tell that you have grown in your responsibilities. Instead of being the person in-charge of organizing all displays and making sure they are in proper order, you instead have the responsibility of overseeing other workers in the completion of this task.

Another key item to keep in mind regarding tense is consistency. Being consistent in your usage is VITAL! If you no longer work at a company, all responsibilities and tasks completed should be in the past tense. You don't want to have an instance where one of your past jobs is using present tense and another is using past. Make sure you review this to make sure that all descriptions are matching. For jobs that you are currently working at, it is fine to have both present and past tense tasks – just make sure you review the tenses to make sure they are in fact appropriate. If this is the case for you, I would recommend having all items in the past tense grouped together so as to make the presentation cleaner and neater.

Formality of Your Writing Style: While writing out your descriptions keep in mind your target audience. This isn't just a simple letter that you are writing out to your friends. Your resume is the first look into what makes you, you. Keep in mind that your future boss(es) will be looking at this as a representation of you. That being said, you want to make sure that your writing style is on the more formal side. Try to avoid using any slang terminology or any words that aren't commonly used. Definitely don't use any shorthanded texting or internet lingo or acronyms. For example, avoid the use of "ur" for "your" or "cuz" for "because."

However, while you are writing you don't need to look up more lengthy words to try to make your words sound "fancier." I don't recommend trying to use a thesaurus to look for different manners to say words that you wouldn't normally use in your everyday speech. There is no need to do this. Chances are the person looking at your resume will not care if you have "confer" instead of "communicate" or "ameliorate" instead of "improve." You are also more likely to use the word you looked up improperly if you are not familiar with it. If you are looking for just a simple version of a word so you aren't constantly repeating yourself, this is okay.

Grammar: The use of proper grammar goes hand in hand with the notion of being consistent with your writing style as expressed above. The biggest issue that I have seen in this area is the conjugation of verb tense – i.e. verbs ending with an –ing, -ed, etc. Make sure that you are being consistent in the verb tense you are using. If you have used the -ing ending for one of your verbs in the sentence, this should be maintained throughout the entire sentence. What do I mean by this? See the examples below:

Incorrect

My responsibilities included cleaning, sorting and maintained an organized clothing rack.

Correct

My responsibilities included clean**ing**, sort**ing** and maintain**ing** an organized clothing rack.

Incorrect

Supervised and training of my staff on new tasks.

Correct

Supervis**ed** and train**ed** my staff on new tasks.

OR

In-charge of supervis**ing** and train**ing** my staff on new tasks.

Another important item to keep in mind is your punctuation. This should also be consistent throughout. Whether or not you want to use punctuation in your bulleted lists is up to you, just be sure you are either always using them or always not. What do I mean by this? See the examples below:

Incorrect

- My responsibilities included cleaning, sorting and maintaining an organized clothing rack.
- I was in charge of updating the weekly schedule
- Reported to my supervisor for items that were out of stock
- Provided quick and courteous customer service.

Correct

- My responsibilities included cleaning, sorting and maintaining an organized clothing rack.
- I was in charge of updating the weekly schedule.
- Reported to my supervisor for items that were out of stock.
- Provided quick and courteous customer service.

OR

- My responsibilities included cleaning, sorting and maintaining an organized clothing rack
- I was in charge of updating the weekly schedule
- Reported to my supervisor for items that were out of stock
- Provided quick and courteous customer service

<u>Know the Industry Style</u>: The industry of the job you are seeking can play a key role in the writing style you choose when updating your resume. If you are new to the industry, are fresh out of college, or making a career change, you want to make sure you take some time to research what a *typical* resume for the industry looks like. This can be done through an internet search for examples of i.e. marketing resumes, accounting resumes, etc. If you are just graduating from school, make use of your career center and talk to them about possible examples of *typical* resumes for the job industry.

What do I mean by a *typical* resume? Based on the industry, there may be an expected writing style. Some common examples would be in the business and marketing industries. If you plan on entering the business industry, then you can expect a clear and concise writing style. You will want to make your point as clearly and briefly as you can. All your writing should be cleanly laid out on the paper, most likely in a standard size 12 font with justified margins. Whereas, writing in a marketing field could be quite the opposite. Generally, the style of writing in this industry is more "free" when compared with the business industry. You won't be expected to have a basic, clean, and simple resume. Instead, it is allowed and, in many places, encouraged, to be a bit more daring with how you present your resume. As you are expected to be a bit more creative in a marketing position, using a business style resume with clear cut lines and quick, concise sentences could set you back from others.

The easiest way to get an idea for how a resume typically looks for the position you are applying is to do a quick internet search. There are hundreds of examples of resumes online that can help you obtain a feel for what might be expected. If you have no idea and are at a complete loss for how to write your resume, don't stress out. The best method to fall back on is the standard business style resume. Having information laid out cleanly and simply is always a good way to go, it just might not set you apart.

Tip #5 – Choose a Suitable Font

An important item that goes hand and hand with the manner in which you decide to write your resume is font choice. There are hundreds of different options and styles out there to choose from. How do you know what style is best? That is a very good question. And one that there is not necessarily any one correct answer. There have been tons of studies done regarding this, each one likely providing a different response. And I'm sure if you ask around your friends for fonts they used, you will either be told that they just used the default font in their word processor or the standard Times New Roman. Again, neither would be wrong.

In this section, I'm going to go into some details surrounding some of the major discussions regarding what to think about when you are choosing your font, provide you with feedback on what I typically think is best, and will provide you with some links to resources and articles that may be helpful when you make the final decision of what font to choose.

Topics of Discussion: A topic that is always, and probably will always be, the biggest discussion regarding font has to do with whether or not you use a font with the "little feet" on them (also known as a serif font) or without the "little feet" (also known as a sans font). Below are some examples of what I mean by this:

Serif Font Examples:
Baskerville Old Face; Bookman Old Style; Century; Garamond; Times New Roman;

Sans Serif Font Examples:
Arial; Calibri; Franklin Gothic; Helveltica Narrow; Verdana;

21

You will notice that the serif fonts have a line under all letters that end in the writing line and that don't curve or fall below this area. Whereas, the sans serif fonts just sort of end or are rounded out. There is no right or wrong answer regarding which font style is better. The general discussion relating to these characteristics generally comes down to a serif font is typically easier to read as your eyes are able to follow the line created by the manner the letters fall, and that a sans serif font typically give your writing a more modern feel and seems to provide a better presentation.

While there is no correct answer as to which type you should use, there is a correct answer when it comes to certain fonts that you should not use in your resume. Fonts that are in cursive are usually good to stay away from (i.e. anything with the word "script" in its name). One reason being – not everyone is able to read cursive, or at least they aren't very good at it. However, the most common reason behind this is that it's just harder to read a cursive font. The letters tend to curve and are typically much closer to each other than you would find in a non-cursive font. You don't want to make someone strain to read, otherwise it could make them lose interest and put your resume down.

Another type of font you want to stay away from would be ones that look too childish (i.e. Comic Sans, Kristen, Tahoma). These fonts will make your resume stand out from the crowd, but not in a manner you would like. Using one of these fonts will make it harder for the person reviewing your resume to take it seriously or, even worse, they may think that you will not take the position you are applying to seriously. Remember, you want to make sure that you are always trying to present yourself through your resume in the manner you would present yourself at work.

My Thoughts: When I am updating my resume or reviewing someone's, there are always two main items that I keep in mind or provide as feedback – (1) stay away from Times New Roman Font, and (2) use a font that has the "little feet."

Why might you ask do I try to stay away from Times New Roman, or recommend that people try out a different font? To put it simply, it just makes the resume feel too "cookie cutter." There are going to be a lot of other applicants who stuck with what they know – that Times New Roman is a standard font, easy to read, and widely accepted. From a visual standpoint, your resume will look just like all the other applicants. There won't be anything eye catching to set you apart.

If you are spending all this time to make sure you are putting on your best impression in your writing style, grammar and previous positions, don't just give up when it comes to the font. Picking font is never fun, particularly since there are so many. However, I feel that it is important to put in a couple extra minutes to test out how different fonts look. This being said – I don't recommend using a font that is in cursive or one of the old fashioned blocked writing. Just keep in mind, I'm not saying that you can't use a font that essentially looks exactly like Times New Roman. Ideally, what you are looking for is a font that is easy to read, looks formal enough (i.e. not Comic Sans), and will set you slightly further apart from the competition. By choosing a not so standard font, there is a chance that someone will notice that you took the extra time to pay attention to some of the more minor details. This never hurts.

My next main item that I usually recommend is to go with a font that has the "little feet" on them. Personally, I find that it is easier to read. It seems like your eyes are more able to follow along and read faster if those little feet are there to help guide them on their way. In addition to this, the font seems more formal with the lines. Sans Serif fonts (or the ones without the little feet) are more commonly found in children's books.

Again, these are my personal preferences and what I usually do or recommend. As long as you are using a font that is legible, easy to read, and doesn't look like it belongs in a children's book, there is no right or wrong answer. The key things you want to keep in mind when you are choosing your font are:

- Does the font make sense based on my audience?

- Is the writing legible?
- Can it be easily read?
- Are the letters too close together or too far apart? (i.e. should I use a standard font or should I use one that provides for a narrow option?)
- Does the font take up too much space / is it too big? (This is important when you are trying to work on the length of your resume. We will get into this a bit later on).

Resources: There have been tons of studies completed relating to what font types are the best to use and for what purposes. No matter how much time you spend looking through all of the resources available, you won't be able to come to an absolute right or wrong answer. For this I say, use all websites as a guide and in the end only you can decide what font you want to use. As the saying goes, trust your gut. It's usually correct. Below are a couple links to various articles that provide some good insight and other recommendations in helping you choose the font:

** Note: I am not sponsored by or affiliated with these sites in any manner. These are just some articles / sites that I came across after writing the section in hopes of providing some additional resources

- "What Font Should I Use?: Five Principles for Choosing and Using Typefaces" by Dan Mayer.
  http://www.smashingmagazine.com/2010/12/what-font-should-i-use-five-principles-for-choosing-and-using-typefaces/
- "The Best Fonts to Use on Your Resume" by Nicole Fallon.
  http://www.businessnewsdaily.com/5331-best-resume-fonts.html
- "Study of Font Styles and Best Uses for Each" by Tara Hornor.
  http://www.instantshift.com/2012/04/12/study-of-font-styles-and-best-uses-for-each/

Tip #6 – Be Sure to Use Action Verbs

When you are finalizing the lists of jobs and responsibilities that you have had, make sure that you have chosen good action verbs in your descriptions. By being selective and thinking about the verbs you are using, you will help to accentuate the tasks that you have completed.

What makes a verb strong v. weak? Let's take a look at some examples below:

Weak	Strong
-Lead, Manage	-Oversee, Mentor, Train
-Clean	-Organize, Maintain
-Run (i.e. Run a department)	-Control, Direct, Oversee
-Update	-Improve, Revise
-Help	-Assist, Facilitate
-Take (i.e. Take various educational classes)	-Attend
-Take (i.e. Take on responsibility)	-Undertake, Assume
-Show	-Demonstrate, Illustrate, Explain
-Learn (i.e. Learn how to)	-Study
-Start	-Implement, Initiate

Using any of the verbs in the right hand column will help to make the tasks and responsibilities you held sound more important. By staying away from the weaker verbs, you will also help to make your resume stand out. You will sound much bolder than other potential candidates. Just be aware - if you plan on using a thesaurus when looking for stronger, bolder words make sure you understand and are familiar with the word that you are putting onto your resume. You want to make sure that the verb makes sense in the context chosen. A strong verb in the wrong context is, more likely than not, worse than just using a weak verb in your resume.

Tip #7 – Proofread, Proofread, Proofread

The most important thing you should keep in mind when you think you have completed your resume is to proofread it! If you have already gone through it and looked it over, put it aside for a day or two, a couple hours, or even twenty minutes. Then go back and take another look at it. Reviewing your resume once is not, and will never be, enough! Always make sure you look at it at least twice. Why do I recommend taking a day or two between when you finish updating your resume and when you should look at it again? This will help you with any bias you have towards yourself and your writing. Let's face it, we're all human. As a result, it's hard to tell ourselves that we messed up or that what we have written is actually not nearly as good or organized as we thought it sounded when we wrote it. Having a day or two break will give you a step back from your writing. This will help you to be a little more objective, and possibly a little harder on yourself, while you review for consistency in grammar or tense. If you don't have the luxury of having a day or two, at least give yourself as much time as possible before you take that second (or even third) look over what you have.

If you have the opportunity, you should definitely take advantage of having an independent party look at your resume. Don't know where to start, or who to ask? Below are some places / resources that you can look into when trying to figure out who is best to review your resume:

Ask Someone Close to You: The easiest place to look for assistance is by asking someone close to you – i.e. a friend or family member. Typically, these individuals are willing to help you out without charging you anything. This is always a good starting point. Ideally, they will be able to help point out any spelling or grammatical errors; however, even if the person isn't very good with grammar, you can always have them take a look at your resume to make sure the fonts look consistent and that your name is spelled correctly. They don't necessarily have to be an English pro to help you out with the small details.

Your College or High School: A lot of schools are more than willing to help out past alumni when it comes to resume reviews. Why you might ask? It's a double benefit. Not only do they get the opportunity to help out one of their former students, but they also receive the added benefit of being able to add you to their statistics of individuals who received a job while attending or after having attended their school. Most schools, regardless of high school or college level, will have you fill out a survey of sorts when you are near graduation to let them know whether you have a job or not. Anything they can do to help increase their statistics will be good for them.

Putting the notion of statistics aside, schools are filled with many resources (teachers / professors) that are good with grammar, and will have the knowledge base to help you catch some items that you might have missed. Or they might just be able to provide suggestions on areas that could use some improvement. If you are able to ask someone at your college or university, this will definitely have an added advantage as most have a career center. There will be someone in the office that is familiar with the different formatting and font styles across the different industries; as a result, they will be able to provide further advice in this regard.

Various Online Sites: Still having trouble finding someone to help you, or think that your resume is not quite right? These days you can find just about anything on the internet, help with your resume is definitely one of them. The best place for your money that I am able to provide reputable feedback for and that I have had personal experience with is the site Fiverr (www.fiverr.com). If you are unfamiliar with this site, people can posts gigs stating tasks that they are willing to complete for $5 – i.e. someone that is willing to review and edit your resume for $5 – or on the flip side, items that you would like someone to complete – i.e. if you wanted someone to create a logo for you, you could create a post to see if there was anyone willing to create one for $5. As you can tell, there is a theme - each gig costs $5. Granted, I am unable to provide reputable feedback for every individual that has a gig posted; however, if you don't know of anyone that seems to be good at grammar this is definitely a good place to start and for a small fee. Even if the person only finds a couple errors, that is still a couple more errors that you would have missed and your employer might have caught.

As you are going through and reviewing your resume, or having your resume reviewed, you want to keep one key thing in mind. You should expect to have at least two errors discovered the first time your resume is being reviewed. Why do I recommend having this in mind? This will help you try to maintain your bias level. Obviously, there is a great chance that there are more than two errors in your resume, however, if you know you need to find at least two errors, then you at least will go into the proofreading mindset without thinking your resume is completely perfect.

Tip #8 – Impressing v. Exaggerating

As you are putting information on your resume – whether it relates to skills, responsibilities or job titles – it is very important to keep in mind and understand the difference between creating a good impression of yourself and position(s), and exaggerating and stretching the truth.

It is very common for individuals to put down items on their resume that aren't fully accurate. Maybe you were the night shift manager for one night when your regular manager was out sick, or maybe you were the night shift manager for a month when your regular manager was being replaced. While you had the experience of being a night shift manager temporarily in both scenarios above, the treatment on your resume should be different for each.

In the first situation, it would be easy to put down that you were the night shift manager – I mean you did do it for one day. But, how much did you actually learn in that one day? While it could be perfectly fine and no one might find out that you only held the position for one day, there are definitely times when exaggerating the truth in this situation could get you into trouble. Should the new company talk with individuals at your old company, it is likely that they will ask questions relating to when you were night shift manager. If your old company doesn't remember this one instance in which you filled in, they may tell the new company that you never were a manager. Believe me, this will definitely put a damper on any excitement to bring you into the new company. However, if you had just stated that you would fill in as necessary as the night shift manager (you don't need to say that this opportunity only arose once), then it would be more likely that your old company in this situation would say it was likely you did take on the role at least once but they cannot remember. This will still keep you in good standing with the new company.

Other instances in which I have seen this occur, or have heard interviewers comment about an interviewee, relates to skills put on your resume. If you have worked in a computer software, i.e. QuickBooks, a couple times several years ago but don't quite remember what the reports are or how to use the software, you may be better off leaving it off your resume or including basic knowledge next to this skill. This instance happened once in my personal experience in which an interviewee had QuickBooks included as a skill on their resume, but when the interviewer started discussing the software and asking questions related to it, the individual was not able to carry on the conversation or answer the questions. You don't want to put yourself into this situation. This then brings everything else on your resume into question as to how much you have tried to exaggerate yourself. Just be careful as to what you are including on your resume and know the limits as to where you are trying to impress / emphasize or exaggerate certain points – they can come back to haunt you at some point.

Tip #9 – Use an Appropriate Length

Length can be a very important detail of your resume. Once a job posting is uploaded, there can be anywhere from one candidate to hundreds of candidates sending in their resumes and cover letters. How exciting does that sound if you were the person in charge of reading, reviewing, and narrowing down the candidate pool? If you have not had the pleasure of going through and sorting resumes, let me tell you it is not a very exciting task. It can be, if you get some good, qualified candidates, but for the most part not so much.

Now imagine if all one hundred candidates sent in resumes that were three pages in length. This task just went from not so much fun, to very daunting. By the last couple resumes, the individual is not going to be as excited to read about the candidates previous experiences. What can you do to help make sure that your resume gets the full attention that it deserves? Use the golden rule – keep your resume as close to one page as possible. If you are older or have been involved with many different positions that are relevant to the one you are applying, there are exceptions to this rule.

If you are struggling to get your resume to be one page, try some of the following:

- Remove previous experiences that don't relate to the position you are applying. For example, if you are applying to a job in a finance position, you could probably delete the blurb you have relating to the two-year period that you were a paper boy five years ago.
- Remove skills or responsibilities that don't relate to the position you are applying.

For example, if you have QuickBooks included on your resume but don't really remember it, you could probably delete this to open up some space.

- Adjust the margins of your resume to make them smaller so more words / characters can fit across. Just make sure you print a test page to verify the style of your resume still looks good.

- Adjust the font size of your resume to make it a little smaller. Just make sure you print a test page to verify the size is still readable and won't cause people to have to squint to read it.

- Adjust the sentences that you have included to describe your previous positions. Maybe instead of using five words to describe something, there is a better verb or simpler manner to state your sentence.

If you find that you are in the position where you cannot get your resume to be one page, you want to try to have the important items that relate to the position you are applying show up as close to page one as possible. When might this occur? This is common if you have been working in various fields, both relevant and not relevant, for over ten years. Or if you have switched places of work multiple times over the past couple years.

If you are still stuck and are unable to find a way to get your resume on one page, or to have the more relevant information presented closer to page one, it may be in your best interest to also include a cover letter. This will allow you to highlight the more important positions, skills, and responsibilities that you have had without having to completely change the flow of your resume.

Tip #10 – Know When a Cover Letter May be the Deciding Factor

Now that you have spent all this time putting together your resume and making sure that it is perfect, you're done right? Possibly. Some places require that you also include a cover letter along with your resume. Why might this be an additional requirement? This letter essentially sums up the items on your resume that you think are important – i.e. most relevant experience – and typically includes a sentence or two on why you believe you would be the best fit for the job, or why you would like to be offered this specific position. However, while a cover letter is not always required, it may be something worth thinking about. This letter can be used as a tool to help you separate yourself from the many others who are applying to the position. Below, I will explain certain situations in which you more likely than not want to include a cover letter, as well as why even if you don't fit into one of these categories, you may want to include one anyways. Please note that I am not going to go into the specifics of what is typically included in a cover letter.

Possible Situations Surrounding your Resume and Cover Letter:
Requirement for Position: This situation is pretty self-explanatory, but I am throwing it in here in case you aren't sure of the consequences. If you are applying for a position and it specifically states that a cover letter is required, be sure to include one with your resume. Should you forget to attach one with your resume and you notice right away, make sure you re-send your resume and cover letter immediately. Any employer will likely just toss aside your resume should it be received without a required cover letter. This will be taken by the employer that you are unable to follow or read directions carefully, and clearly any employer will not

want to spend their time on you when there are several other candidates who are able to follow the directions.

Applying to a Position in Another State / County: If you are planning on moving to another state, or even a town that is a couple hours away from where you currently live, it can be very difficult to obtain an interview if you don't already have an address in that specific location. Many employers are afraid that either (1) you may change your mind about the move after they have spent the time interviewing you and preparing your offer, or (2) that you will expect them to help you with your relocation costs. Should this scenario meet your situation, then I definitely recommend the inclusion of a cover letter with your resume. You will want to state in the letter your plans and intentions for getting to the area and that you are not expecting any relocation costs (if you are hoping for relocation reimbursement, I would leave this out of your letter). By including this letter, you will help your chances of having your resume reviewed as your plan will be plainly laid out without the employer having to contact you first.

Over or Underqualified for Position: At times when your previous experience, certifications or educational background may either set you ahead of or behind the skill requirements the employer is looking for, a cover letter may also be a good route to go. Typically, if you are overqualified, an employer will be afraid to hire you since they fear you will want a much higher salary than what they are willing to pay. If you are underqualified, an employer will be afraid that you will set yourself and your co-workers up for failure if you don't pick up the tasks, software, etc. quick enough. Through the use of a cover letter, you will be able to outline that you are aware of the potential salary adjustment from what you are used to (for overqualified candidates), or what you are willing to do in order to make up for the lack of skills as required in the job description (for underqualified candidates). By doing this, you may be able to reduce some of the fear and help ease the employer's mind.

Career Change: Making a career change goes hand and hand with the items noted above in the over or underqualified section above. Looking at your resume alone, an employer will be confused as to why you are applying to, say for example, a career in accounting if all your previous experiences were in the field of finance or biology. In your letter, you will want to outline what you are willing to do to meet any requirements of the job. You will also want to explain that you are looking to make a jump in industries and outline how you can take your previous experiences to help benefit your new position.

Looking for a Way to Stand Out: You always have the option of writing a cover letter just because, with no actual situation or dilemma that you need to explain. A cover letter can be used as a tool to help set you apart from the other applicants. It provides you with an arena in which you can explain why you want the position and how your previous experiences will help you excel in this new position. Some employers like seeing cover letters as they are able to see the items that you believe are important about the position, your character and experiences.

Now, after reading all of the items discussed above, you may be thinking that all of that makes sense and I can see how it may help, but is it really still worth the time? The answer is, it depends. Honestly, there are some people who don't want to have to look at an additional page of information that they need to sort through and read. However, I feel like these individuals are not as common when it comes to resumes. In my interview process, I have found that many people involved in the interviewing and recruiting like when they receive a cover letter attached to a resume. Not only does it show that the applicant went the extra, not required step to take the time to actually put their thoughts into words and sentences, but, as mentioned above, it provides a summary. You are able to review this one sheet of paper and gain a better feel of whether someone will fit into a company than you would by looking at a resume.

It also points out the main items so the individual won't necessarily need to spend as much time looking over your resume in full detail.

Personally, I have been told before by an interviewer that they were thoroughly impressed that I had included a cover letter along with my resume when it wasn't required. They went on to explain that this helped me stand apart from the competition and moved me up on the list of potential candidates to interview. That being said – my opinion is that if you have time and think it will help you stand out, you should take the extra time to include a cover letter. Just be sure that there is nothing on the listing that states to not include one. If you are working with a recruiter, I would ask them if they are aware of the company's preferences regarding cover letters. Also, don't include one just to include one. Make sure that you are taking the time and effort to write one, and write it well. If you write your cover letter and find that it just sounds like a bunch of fluff and you have nothing to add to supplement your resume, don't include it.

Conclusion

Hopefully after reading through all of these tips you now feel ready to prepare and submit an outstanding resume. Keep in mind that you want to look into the position you are applying to, come up with a list of previous positions and what you did in those positions, and describe them with relevant and strong actions verbs.

Always, always proofread your resume before you are submitting it anywhere. If you are submitting a cover letter along with your resume, make sure that the company name is spelled correctly!

As I said before, it's very important that you stay true to who you are and your skills while writing your resume and cover letter. Creating a good impression of yourself is fine, but don't try to exaggerate or add too much emphasis on an area that you aren't fully certain about; it will come out at some point that you do not have the expertise in this area, and this will not look good on your part.

Now go on out there and start applying!

Appendix A

Examples of List of Jobs / Volunteer Activities

Name of Retail Store

Sales Associate

January 20X0 – August 20X1

- Worked register
- Customer service
- Organized store
- Took inventory

Name of Restaurant

Waiter / Food Server

August 20X1 – September 20X2

- Customer service
- Kept customers happy
- Managed multiple tables
- Kept area clean and organized

High School Store

Volunteer Sales Associate

September 20X2 – December 20X2

- Worked register
- Customer service

Nanny / Babysitter

January 20X3 – May 20X3

- Created schedules

- Cared for two children, aged five years old and three years old (at the time of starting)
- Prepared and served meals and snacks
- Bathed and dressed the children
- Organized games and story time

Name of Non-Profit Organization

Treasurer

September 20X2 – May 20X3

- Created schedules
- Prepared financial statements
- Kept receipts

Name of Non-Profit Organization

Member

September 20X2 – May 20X3

- Attended events
- Helped organize events

Appendix B

Examples of Items to List for Skills

- Microsoft Office Suite – Advanced level
- Outlook – Basic level
- Quickbooks – Intermediate level
- Spanish – Fluent
- Portuguese – Basic
- Leadership training – Have attended multiple seminars
- Certified in CPR – Obtained in February 20X1
- Certified lifeguard – Obtained in February 20X1
- ServSafe certified – Obtained May 20X1
- Strong verbal and written communication
- Very patient
- Attentive to details
- Can type X WPM
- Delegates effectively
- Meets deadlines
- Manages social media campaigns
- Organization and prioritization skills
- Self-motivated
- Knows when to take initiative
- Ability to work under pressure

Appendix C

Examples of Items to Keep in Mind While Reviewing the Company Website

- What are the educational qualifications for the position? Do I meet these? If not, would I be willing to take the time to meet these qualifications?
- Are there any previous job experience requirements? Do I meet all of these or some? (I.e. if it says 5 years experience, do I at least have a year of experience?)
- Is the salary reasonable compared to what I was hoping, or within reason to negotiate?
- What are the key duties or responsibilities required to complete the job? Would I have any issues, physically or mentally, in completing any of these tasks?
- Do I understand what all of the key duties or responsibilities listed are and what would be expected of me, or do I need more information?
- Are there any special technical skills required to complete the job? Would I have any issues, physically or mentally, in completing any of these tasks? Would I be willing to take the time to learn any new technical skills?
- What type of services does the Company offer? Do I have any background knowledge in these areas? If not, do these services intrigue / interest me at all? Would I be willing to take classes or put in an effort to learn about these areas?

- In what industries does the Company do business? Do I have any background knowledge in these areas? If not, do these industries intrigue / interest me at all? Would I be willing to take classes or put in an effort to learn about these areas?

Appendix D

Examples of Questions to Ask About a Job Position

- Could you please explain what a typical routine would be for someone in this position?
- Is this a full-time or part-time position?
- How many hours are expected? Is overtime expected?
- How much travel will be expected?
- What type of software is used in the position? Is there on-the-job training or other courses that can be taken to learn the software?
- What kind of training programs will be available when I start?
- How is performance evaluated?
- Is there potential for growth in the Company? Are there possibilities for promotion?
- Will the tasks performed be similar on a daily basis? Or will there be a variety in the tasks completed?
- What kind of authority does the position have?
- How many people will I be working with?
- Would I be managing any other employees?
- How would you describe the responsibilities of the position? Which skill / responsibility is the most important for the completion of the job?
- What do you consider to be the most important aspect of the job?
- What tools or resources are available to assist with being successful in this position?
- When the listing says [insert item from listing], could you please explain further as to what this means?

- When the listing says [insert item from listing], could you please provide me with an example of what is meant by this?
- Is there anything else you think I need to know?
- Who else would you recommend I speak with? When I call, may I use your name?

www.ingramcontent.com/pod-product-compliance
Lightning Source LLC
Chambersburg PA
CBHW070921180526
45168CB00005B/2103